P...
Ca...

The Support Assets

by Pamela Espeland and Elizabeth Verdick

free spirit
PUBLISHING®

Helping kids
help themselves™
since 1983

Library of Congress Cataloging-in-Publication Data
Espeland, Pamela
    People who care about you: the support assets / by Pamela Espeland and Elizabeth Verdick.
        p. cm. — (The "Adding assets" series for kids; bk. 1)
    Includes index.
    ISBN 1-57542-162-3
1. Children—Social networks—Juvenile literature. 2. Security (Psychology) in
children—Juvenile literature. 3. Family—Psychological aspects—Juvenile literature.
4. Caring—Juvenile literature. I. Verdick, Elizabeth. II. Title. III. Series.
    HQ784.S56E87 2004
        305.23—dc22

                                                                                    2004009871

Search Institute℠ and Developmental Assets™ are trademarks of Search Institute.

The original framework of 40 Developmental Assets (for adolescents) was developed by Search Institute © 1997, Minneapolis, MN 1-800-888-7828; *www.search-institute.org*. The Developmental Assets framework is used under license from Search Institute.

The FACTS! (pages 8, 21, 34, 45, 58, and 68) are from *Coming into Their Own: How Developmental Assets Promote Positive Growth in Middle Childhood* by Peter C. Scales, Arturo Sesma Jr., and Brent Bolstrom (Minneapolis: Search Institute, 2004).

Illustrated by Chris Sharp
Cover design by Marieka Heinlen
Interior design by Crysten Puszczykowski
Index by Ina Gravitz

10 9 8 7 6 5 4 3 2 1
Printed in the United States of America

Free Spirit Publishing Inc.
217 Fifth Avenue North, Suite 200
Minneapolis, MN 55401-1299
(612) 338-2068
help4kids@freespirit.com
www.freespirit.com

Contents

Introduction

If you knew ways to make your life better, right now and for the future, would you try them?

We're guessing you would, and that's why we wrote this book. It's part of a series of eight books called the **Adding Assets Series for Kids.**

What Are Assets, Anyway?

When we use the word **assets**, we mean good things you need in your life and yourself.

We don't mean houses, cars, property, and jewelry—assets whose value is measured in money. We mean **Developmental Assets** that help you to be and become your best. Things like a close, loving family. A neighborhood where you feel safe. Adults you look up to and respect. And (sorry!) doing your homework.

There are 40 Developmental Assets in all. This book is about adding six of them to your life. They're called the **Support Assets** because they're about having *people* around you who love you, care for you, appreciate you, and accept you. They're about having *places* to be and go where you feel safe, supported, and welcome.

The Support Assets

Asset Name	What It Means
Family Support	You feel loved and supported in your family.
Positive Family Communication	You and your parent(s) can talk to each other. You feel comfortable asking your parent(s) for advice.
Other Adult Relationships	Other adults besides your parent(s) give you support and encouragement.
Caring Neighborhood	You have neighbors who know you and care about you.
Caring School Climate	You get along well with teachers and other kids at your school. You feel that school is a caring, encouraging place to be.
Parent Involvement in Schooling	Your parents are actively involved in helping you succeed in school.

Other books in the series are about the other 34 assets.* That may seem like a lot, but don't worry. You don't have to add them all at once. You don't have to add them in any particular order. But the sooner you can add them to your life, the better.

---

* If you're curious to know what the other assets are, you can read the whole list on pages 82–83.

Why You Need Assets

An organization called Search Institute surveyed hundreds of thousands of kids and teens across the United States. Their researchers found that some kids have a fairly easy time growing up, while others don't. Some kids get involved in harmful behaviors or dangerous activities, while others don't.

What makes the difference? Developmental Assets! Kids who have them are more likely to do well. Kids who don't have them are less likely to do well.

Maybe you're thinking, "Why should I have to add my own assets? I'm just a kid!" Because kids have the power to make choices in their lives. You can choose to sit back and wait for other people to help you, or you can choose to help yourself. You can also work with other people who care about you and want to help.

Many of the ideas in this book involve working with other people—like your parents, grandparents, aunts, uncles, and other family grown-ups. And your teachers, neighbors, coaches, Scout leaders, and religious leaders. They can all help add assets for you and with you.

It's likely that many of the adults in your life are already helping. In fact, an adult probably gave you this book to read.

How to Use This Book

Start by choosing **one** asset to add. Read the stories at the beginning and end of that chapter. The stories are examples of the assets in everyday life. Then pick **one** idea and try it. See how it goes. After that, try another idea, or move on to another asset.

Don't worry about being perfect or getting it right. Know that by trying, you're doing something great for yourself.

The more assets you add, the better you'll feel about yourself and your future. Soon you won't be a kid anymore. You'll be a teenager. Because you have assets, you'll feel and be a lot more sure of yourself. You'll make better decisions. You'll have a head start on success.

We wish you the very best as you add assets to your life.

Pamela Espeland and Elizabeth Verdick
Minneapolis, MN

A Few Words About Families

Kids today live in many different kinds of families.

Maybe you live with one or both of your parents. Maybe you live with other adult relatives—aunts and uncles, grandparents, grown-up brothers or sisters or cousins.

Maybe you live with a stepparent, foster parent, or guardian. Maybe you live with one of your parents and his or her life partner.

In this series, we use the word **parents** to describe the adults who care for you in your home. We also use **family adults**, **family grown-ups**, and **adults at home**. When you see any of these words, think of your own family, whatever kind it is.

Family Support

What it means: You feel loved and supported in your family.

Sam's Story "Hey, guys, it's game night, so we're eating early," Sam's stepmom says from the kitchen.

Sam's little sister Lindsey jumps up and yells, "Mac and cheese! Cool! C'mon, Sam!" But Sam doesn't budge from in front of the TV.

"Sam," Mom says, louder this time, "come to the table. We've got to be at the school gym in an hour. That doesn't give us much time to eat, get ready, and drive there."

"Just drop me off tonight, Mom," Sam answers, still staring at the TV. "You don't have to stay for the game. I can get a ride home with Coach Miller."

Dad walks in the door. "Hi, everybody!" he calls out. "I'm home early so I can support the Panthers tonight."

Sam stands up and shouts, "What's the point? Why would you want to watch me mess up and look like a fool?"

"Whoa," Dad says. "What's going on?"

Lindsey puts her hands on her hips and announces, "Sam's mad 'cause the Panthers have been losing so much that kids at school call them the Pukers."

"Shut up, birdbrain!" Sam yells, throwing his empty juice box.

Click. The TV goes off. Sam turns and sees Mom holding the remote, looking furious. Keeping her voice calm, she says, "Family meeting. Kitchen table. On the double."

Sam has the *Family Support* asset, even at times when he thinks he doesn't deserve it.

Think about your own life. Do you feel loved and supported in your family?

If **YES,** keep reading to learn ways to make this asset even stronger.

If **NO,** keep reading to learn ways to add this asset to your life.

You can also use these ideas to help add this asset for other people—like your friends, family members, neighbors, and kids at school.

Facts!

Kids with the *Family Support* asset:

✔ have higher self-esteem

✔ are better at making and keeping friends

✔ are less likely to get into arguments or fights

ways to Add This Asset

 **AT HOME**

Try Some QT. Does your family mostly spend time together doing errands and watching TV? There's nothing wrong with that, but you could be doing MORE. How about some QT (Quality Time)? Even as little as 15 minutes now and then can make a big difference.

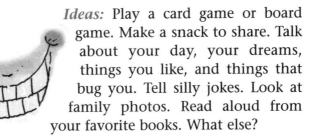

Ideas: Play a card game or board game. Make a snack to share. Talk about your day, your dreams, things you like, and things that bug you. Tell silly jokes. Look at family photos. Read aloud from your favorite books. What else?

4 Quick Ideas for More QT

1. Eat dinner together with the TV off.
2. Get up 20 minutes earlier so you can eat breakfast together.
3. Talk when you're riding in the car or on the bus. Take off the headphones and turn off the hand-held video game.
4. Go for walks together. Around the block, to the park and back, to the corner store, wherever. Once a day, twice a week, or whenever you can fit it in. Walking is QT with a bonus: exercise!

Remember I♥U. Some families say "I love you" like it's the most natural thing in the world. But a lot of families have trouble with those three little words. Maybe you can start a new tradition of using more "love" words at home. If you feel funny doing this face to face, start with a note or an email. There are lots of ways to say you care—like "Love ya!" "You're the greatest!" and "I♥U!"

Hug and Be Hugged. Physical touch—a hug, a kiss, a friendly pat—is a great way to show love and support. But what if your family isn't into all that mushy stuff? Start small. *Ideas:* Put your arm around your mom when you're sitting together on the couch. Slip your hand into your dad's hand as you take a walk. Give your sister or brother a high five before leaving for school, or try a quick hug as you run out the door.

TIP: If your parents are the huggy, kissy type and you feel weird when they show you affection in front of your friends, say so—but be nice. Try setting a few small rules, like: "No kissing me at the bus stop, okay?" or "Please, let's NOT hug at the mall!" Your parents will probably understand. You're not saying you NEVER want them to touch you—just not when your friends are around.

Be Supportive. Think about how you like to be treated, then treat your family members the same. *Example:* If you see a family member doing a chore—like cooking, cleaning, or yard work—offer to help. Don't wait to be asked. (Wouldn't you love it if someone offered to help you clean your room?) *Another example:* If a family member looks sad, ask if they want to talk. Then listen when they do. *X-Treme example:* You've got plans to spend the afternoon at a friend's house. Then you notice that your little sister is struggling with her math homework. You call your friend, stay home, and help your sister. (And become her hero for life.)

Give Positive Feedback. Everyone likes to be noticed for the good things they do. Everyone likes to be thanked. The next time a family adult helps you feel loved and supported, say something! *Examples:* "Thanks for helping with my school project, Mom. I couldn't have done it without you." "I love coming to your house after school, Grandma. Plus you always have cookies. You're the best grandma in the whole world!"

Want It? Ask for It! Your parents can't read your mind (which is a good thing, if you think about it). That's why it's important to tell them what you need. This doesn't mean begging for the latest CD. It means asking for support in specific ways. *Examples:* "Dad, can we spend more time together when you get home from work? I know you've been busy, but I really miss just being with you." "Mom, I have a problem. Can I talk to you tonight?" If you have trouble saying the words out loud, you could write a note.

A message for you

What if your family doesn't provide the love and support you need? What if you feel you can't talk to your parents? Try talking with another adult you trust. What about a teacher? A school counselor? A neighbor? Your best friend's dad or mom? An adult at your place of worship? Maybe that person can help you figure out how to talk to your parents. Or maybe that person can give you some of the support you're not getting at home.

 AT SCHOOL

★ Take part in family events at your school, like open houses and family nights. Be sure to let your parents know when these events will happen. That way, you can all plan to go.

★ Come up with more ideas for family events at your school. What about a spaghetti dinner once a month? A pancake breakfast some Saturday morning? A family movie night? Share your ideas with a teacher or your school principal.

IN YOUR NEIGHBORHOOD

★ Find out what your community is doing for families. Look in your local newspaper. When you're out with your parents, check the bulletin boards at your community center, public library, or nearby coffee shop. Is there something coming up that you could all enjoy together? What about a free concert? A nature walk? Family Day at a zoo or museum? A read-a-thon at the library? Spend time in your community as a family.

IN YOUR FAITH COMMUNITY

★ Most faith communities have special programs for families. See what yours offers, then get involved. Does it hold family retreats? Are there chances to volunteer together? *Example:* Some congregations host Thanksgiving dinners for homeless people. Whole families show up to welcome guests, serve food, and clean tables.

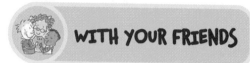

WITH YOUR FRIENDS

★ Tell each other about ways you feel loved and supported in your family. What has your dad or mom done lately to help you feel that way? It could be a big thing, like Mom cutting short a business trip so she wouldn't miss one of your games. It could be a small thing, like Dad putting a note in your backpack saying, "Good luck on your spelling test!!!"

Start Adding!

Pick at least ONE idea you've read here and give it a try. Then think about or write about what happened. Will you try another idea to help build more love and support in your family?

Back to Sam's Story Sam and his family sit down at the table, and Lindsey helps herself to a huge pile of macaroni and cheese. Sam glares at her.

"What?" she asks. "I'm hungry, okay?"

"So, what's going on here, Sammy?" Dad asks.

"Dad, the Panthers have lost eight games so far. That's every single game. I'm no good at basketball! I want you guys to stop coming to my games 'cause then you won't see what losers we are!"

"You aren't *losers,*" Mom says. "You're just not winning right now."

"Big difference," Sam mumbles.

"Listen, Sam," Dad says. "We want to be there for you no matter what—that's just the way it is with us."

"Yeah, Sammy," Lindsey adds, with her mouth full of food. *"Hello,* we're your *family*—we don't care if you stink."

Sam gives a grudging smile. "Okay, fine, I get it. I guess I want you to be there, even if we're the worst team in Panther history." Then he digs into dinner.

For a moment or two, no one talks. They're too busy chewing. Then Sam takes a gulp of milk, puts down his glass, and says, "Thanks for your support." He realizes he really means it.

"Look what I got today," Dad says, grinning. He holds up a big foam finger with "#1" printed on it. "What do you guys think? Too much?"

Mom groans. "Yeah, too much—even for us."

Positive Family Communication

What it means: You and your parent(s) can talk to each other. You feel comfortable asking your parent(s) for advice.

Jayde's Story

Jayde's mom calls herself "The Queen of Multi-tasking." Her mom talks on the cell phone while folding sheets, watching the news, and yelling at Jayde to get going on her homework.

Even though her mom gave herself the Queen nickname as a joke, Jayde isn't laughing. It seems as if her mom never pays much attention to Jayde and only has time for work, chores, and paying bills.

Jayde's older sister Tessa just rolls her eyes about Mom and says to Jayde, "Get used to it." But Jayde doesn't want things to be this way. She wants a mom she can talk to and feel close to.

Jayde doesn't feel that she has the *Positive Family Communication* asset.

Facts!

Kids with the *Positive Family Communication* asset:

✓ feel less lonely

✓ get better grades in school

✓ are more likely to solve problems peacefully

Think about your own life. Do you feel that you and your parents (or other family grown-ups) can talk to each other? Are you comfortable asking them for advice?

If **YES,** keep reading to learn ways to make this asset even stronger.

If **NO,** keep reading to learn ways to add this asset to your life.

You can also use these ideas to help add this asset for other people—like your friends, family members, neighbors, and kids at school.

ways to Add This Asset

 **AT HOME**

Talk, Talk, Talk. Do your parents ask you the same old questions every day? Like "How was school?" and "Did you learn anything today?" Try not to give the same old answers—like "Fine" or "No" or zzzzzz. Instead, tell your dad or mom something funny, annoying, weird, or wonderful that happened during school or sports. Your parents mean well by asking, and talking to them is a great way to connect. *P.S.* How about asking *them* about *their* day?

Remember That Parents Are People, Too. It's hard to imagine your parents as anything other than . . . parents. Believe it or not, they had a life before you arrived. Find out what they were like as kids. What did they do for fun? What were their hobbies? Who were their friends? Ask them to tell you stories about their worst teachers or favorite pets. Look at your parents' old photos and yearbooks. You might discover some cool or interesting things.

TIP: If your mom or dad can't talk to you when you need to be heard, find other adults you can trust. Ask a neighbor, another family adult, a teacher, or a youth group leader. Don't keep your problems and feelings locked up inside. There's someone out there who can help. Keep looking!

Talk About the Hard Stuff. It may not be easy to approach family grown-ups about problems you're having in school or with friends. But they may be better listeners than you think. Wait for a time when things are quiet and calm. Then say something like this: "I have a problem I need help with. Can I tell you about it?"

4 Tips for Talking with Parents

1. Choose a good time. If your parents are busy, tired, or grumpy, wait. Not sure if it's a good time? You can always ask.

2. Keep your voice, words, and body language respectful. That means no yelling, whining, glaring, swearing, slouching, eye-rolling, finger-pointing, or foot-stomping.

3. Look at them when you talk and when they talk (instead of staring at the floor or out the window). Making eye contact helps people communicate.

4. Finish with a "thank you" so everyone leaves with a good feeling.

Tip: If you fight with your brothers and sisters a lot, talk with a family grown-up.

Be There for Your Sisters and Brothers. If you're an older sibling, you're lucky. You get to be a good listener and a Giver of Wise Advice. If you're a younger sibling, you're lucky, too. You have someone older and (hopefully) wiser to talk to. If you need advice or help, go to your older brother or sister. See if he or she has ever dealt with the same issue. This is a great way to build a stronger relationship.

A message for you

Not all kids have siblings. There are plenty of onlies out there. If you're one, maybe your friends are jealous. You don't have to share a room, and you get all of your parents' attention. On the other hand, you may want a family member to talk to—someone closer to your age. What about cousins? Do you have an older cousin who's willing to be like a big brother or sister to you? Can you be a Giver of Wise Advice to a younger cousin or two?

See It from Another Point of View. Sometimes family members argue (big surprise). And sometimes when you argue, it's hard to see anything but your own point of view. You want to win; you want to be *right*. If this happens, take a time-out from the argument and cool off. Think about what the other person was saying. Is there a teeny, tiny chance that you might be wrong? Saying the words, "You know, you might be right," is a great way to make peace.

AT SCHOOL

★ Create a personal portfolio that you can bring home to show your parents. A portfolio is a collection of assignments you've finished, tests you've taken, drawings you've done, and anything else that shows what you're learning and doing in school. All you need is a folder or notebook to store it all in. Bring home your portfolio every week or once a month. Share it with your parents. Talk about how school is going for you.

IN YOUR NEIGHBORHOOD

★ When you're out in public with your family, try to be on your best behavior with each other. No whining, yelling, pouting, or tantrums. (That goes for grown-ups, too!) You might come up with a secret sign you can use when things heat up. *Ideas:* Quietly say "Cooooool it!" Plug your nose. Flap your arms like a chicken. Whatever works! As soon as someone gives the sign, you all go back to your best behavior.

IN YOUR FAITH COMMUNITY

★ Does your faith community have get-togethers especially for parents and kids? If it doesn't, maybe you can get the ball rolling. Ask your religion teacher or youth group leader to help you. *Ideas:* What about a potluck dinner? A games night? An overnight outing? What about starting a discussion group just for parents and kids? You can talk about a different topic each time. If you plan the topics in advance, you can invite experts from your congregation or community to lead the discussions.

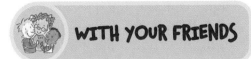

WITH YOUR FRIENDS

★ The next time you're at a friend's house, do a little detective work. (No, this doesn't mean looking through their medicine cabinet or drawers.) Pay attention to how your friend's family communicates. Do the kids talk to the adults? Do the adults talk to the kids? Do they seem to have a great relationship, or a not-so-great relationship? Can you learn anything you might try with your own family?

Start Adding!

Pick at least ONE idea you've read here and give it a try. Then think about or write about what happened. Will you try another idea to help you and your parents talk to each other?

Back to
Jayde's
Story
It takes some courage, but Jayde decides she's going to talk to her mom about what's going on at home. She picks a time when her mom seems calm and isn't doing a zillion things at once.

"Mom," she says, "can we talk about something?"

Her mom replies, "Sure. Come with me into the kitchen and we'll talk while I unload the dishwasher."

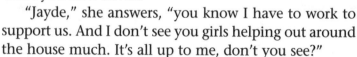

"No, wait," Jayde says. "I mean, that's what I want to talk about. I wish we could just talk and not always be doing something else at the same time. Mom, you're always so busy! Can't you slow down?"

"Jayde," she answers, "you know I have to work to support us. And I don't see you girls helping out around the house much. It's all up to me, don't you see?"

Suddenly Jayde *does* see. Instead of feeling mad or hurt, she gives her mom a hug. Jayde thinks, "I want my mom to be there for me, so I'm going to be there for her."

"Let's unload the dishwasher together," Jayde says. "That way, it'll go faster."

Her mom looks at Jayde and says, "You know what? The dishwasher can wait. Let's sit down and you can tell me all about school. Then you can help me, okay? I'd like that."

Jayde smiles. "Me, too."

Other Adult Relationships

What it means: Other adults besides your parent(s) give you support and encouragement.

Matt & Allie's Story

Matt knows he's lucky. His grandparents live only a few miles from his family's apartment. Two of his aunts and uncles—plus a bunch of cousins—live in his hometown.

After church on Sundays, everyone gathers at Grandma's for brunch. If his mom or stepdad can't bring him to basketball practice, there's usually some other family member who's glad to do it. When he's struggling with math, he gets on the phone to Aunt Sheila, who's good at numbers and loves to help.

But Matt is worried. He sees that his friend, Allie, is having problems at home. She always comes to school looking tired. The other day, she said she couldn't get her social studies homework done because it was too noisy with her mom and dad screaming at each other.

Matt asks Allie, "Is there another grown-up in your family who can help?" When she shakes her head no, he says, "How about coming over after school and talking with my stepdad? His job is helping kids with problems, but he's also good to talk to when you just need someone to listen."

Matt has the *Other Adult Relationships* asset, but Allie doesn't.

Think about your own life. Are there other adults you know—besides your parents—who give you support and encouragement?

If **YES**, keep reading to learn ways to make this asset even stronger.

If **NO**, keep reading to learn ways to add this asset to your life.

You can also use these ideas to help add this asset for other people—like your friends, family members, neighbors, and kids at school.

Facts!

Kids with the *Other Adult Relationships* asset:

✓ feel better about themselves

✓ have fewer behavior problems

✓ are less likely to make friends who are troublemakers

ways to Add This Asset

AT HOME

Stay in Touch. Do you have an address book? If not, you can get one (cheap) or make one (easy—index cards in a box will work). Or keep your address book

TiP: Grown-ups *love* getting handwritten notes or cards from kids. They'll probably save the ones you send them.

on a computer. Write the names, addresses, phone numbers, and email addresses of the important people in your life. Be sure to include the adults who give you support and encouragement. Then use your address book to stay in touch. Write letters, send cards, dash off a quick email, or pick up the phone.

Make a List. Write the names of adults you look up to and want to know better. What about a teacher at your school? One of your friends' parents? Your religious leader or youth group leader? Who else? Once you've made your list, circle **one** name. During the next week or two, do **one** thing to reach out to that person. *Examples:* Thank a teacher for a class or lesson you really enjoyed. Thank a friend's parent for making you feel welcome in their home. Ask your religious leader or youth group leader for advice. Next time, pick another name from your list. You can always add new names.

A message for you

Some kids have large, close families who live nearby. They have plenty of chances to form strong relationships with adults besides their parents. That's not true for all kids, or even most kids these days. Families are a lot more scattered than they used to be. You may have relatives in other states, even other countries. Or you may not have any relatives beyond your immediate family. Don't let that stop you from adding this asset to your life. Are there people your parents hang around with? Friends who are as close to them as family—maybe closer? You might look here for grown-ups you can get to know.

Get Serious. Maybe you've identified a few adults in your life that you know and trust. But do your conversations only touch the surface? *Example:* Maybe you've told them you love pre-Algebra and Scouts, and that you got a new skateboard for your birthday. But did you mention the big fight you had with your best friend last week? Or the crush you have on that girl or boy down the street? You may think that the adults you know won't get that kind of stuff . . . but they will. They've had best-friend fights and crushes themselves (about a million years ago). Give them a chance to listen and learn more about your life.

Ask Your Parents if You Can Get a Mentor. A mentor is a caring adult who's willing to guide you, advise you, and spend time with you. He or she serves as a role model and may become a trusted friend. Many communities and religious organizations have mentoring programs. So do several national organizations, like Big Brothers Big Sisters, Boys and Girls Clubs, the YMCA and YWCA, and Communities in Schools. To find out more, give them a call (check your local phone book) or visit their Web sites (see page 38). To learn more about mentoring in general, visit the National Mentoring Partnership site. There's a whole section on how to find a mentor, and a page where you can search for a program in your area by entering your ZIP code.

Check Them Out Online

★ Big Brothers Big Sisters of America: *www.bbbsa.org*

★ Boys & Girls Clubs of America: *www.bgca.org*

★ Communities in Schools: *www.cisnet.org*

★ National Mentoring Partnership: *www.mentoring.org*

★ YMCA: *www.ymca.net*

★ YWCA: *www.ywca.org*

At School

★ Join a team, group, or club that interests you. Get to know the adult coaches or club leaders.

★ Stay in touch with teachers, even when you change homerooms or move on to the next grade. If you change schools, keep in touch with former teachers by email or snail mail.

IN YOUR NEIGHBORHOOD

★ It's easy to forget that your neighbors aren't just the kids who live next door, down the hall, or on your block, but the *adults* as well. Ask your parents to introduce you to your grown-up neighbors. After that, whenever you see them outside sweeping the porch, planting flowers, or walking the dog, smile and say hello. When neighbors come to visit your dad or mom, don't just mumble hi and disappear. Stick around and visit for a while.

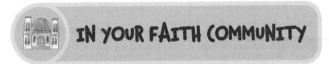

IN YOUR FAITH COMMUNITY

★ Get to know some of the grown-ups in your faith community. *Idea:* Do people gather after worship for coffee and juice and cookies? Instead of hanging out with your friends, introduce yourself to an adult or two. Or spend time talking with one you've already met.

> **TiP:** Your faith community can be a great place to find a mentor.

WITH YOUR FRIENDS

★ The next time you want to bring a friend home for dinner, think about including one of your friend's parents, too. It might be fun to have a mother-daughter or father-son—or any other combination—evening, where you all get to know each other a little better.

Start Adding!

Pick at least ONE idea you've read here and give it a try. Then think about or write about what happened. Will you try another idea to get to know and trust other adults in your life?

Back to
Matt
& Allie's
Story

Matt brings Allie home to talk to his step-dad, Paul. Allie says that her parents fight a lot, and that she has heard the word "divorce" come up when they argue.

Paul listens to Allie. Then he says, "How about if we make a list? We're going to list the other adults in your life that you know and trust."

"But there's no one," Allie says.

"Okay, how about a teacher?" Paul asks. "Or do you play a sport? Is there a coach you can talk to?" Allie says she likes her homeroom teacher a lot, and her soccer coach once said that anyone who needed to talk could knock on her office door anytime.

"That's great!" Paul says. "Write down their names." He hands Allie a piece of paper and a pencil. "Now, what about relatives? Does anyone live near you?" Allie says that she and her grandpa stay in touch through email, and that her favorite older cousin is away at college but still calls to see how Allie is doing.

Allie's list has four names on it already, but they don't stop there. Pretty soon, Allie realizes she has lots of adults she can go to for help: her youth group leader, the school counselor, and Mrs. Gutzman next door. Then Paul says, "Hey, don't forget to put my name on your list!"

Caring Neighborhood

What it means: You have neighbors who know you and care about you.

Lucia's Story

Lucia just moved to a new city—one that's much bigger than where she grew up. She misses her old street so much she can hardly stand it. Everyone there knew everyone else. All the kids had gone to the same school since they were little, and the moms, dads, and other family grown-ups knew all the kids' names.

Lucia had even had the same baby-sitter for as long as she could remember. Instead of going to an after-school program, she always went to Mrs. Alvarez's house, where she stayed until one of her parents came to get her after work.

Now, at her new home on the new street in the new city, Lucia doesn't know anybody. She used to be able to go outside and find someone to play with right away, but not anymore. Back home, there was always a softball or kickball game going on in someone's

43

yard—not here. Plus all the kids felt safe, because someone's parents were always watching out for them. If a kid fell off a bicycle, it took about a second before a parent ran out a door.

Lucia sighs. Everything here is just too new. She feels like a stranger in her own home—in her own bedroom. She wonders if things will ever feel the same again.

Lucia used to have the *Caring Neighborhood* asset, and she misses it a lot.

Facts!

Kids with the *Caring Neighborhood* asset:

✓ feel less lonely

✓ get along better with others

✓ do better in school

Think about your own life. Do you have neighbors who know you and care about you?

If **YES**, keep reading to learn ways to make this asset even stronger.

If **NO**, keep reading to learn ways to add this asset to your life.

You can also use these ideas to help add this asset for other people—like your friends, family members, neighbors, and kids at school.

Ways to Add This Asset

 **AT HOME**

Welcome New Neighbors. Did someone just move in across the street, down the block, or down the hall? Go with a family grown-up to say hi and introduce yourselves. *Ideas:* Sweeten your welcome with a plate of homemade cookies or brownies, or some fresh-picked flowers from your yard. Bring along a welcome card signed by other neighbors.

Make a Map. Draw your neighborhood—whatever
that means to you and your family. This may be one
block with a lot of buildings, or many streets with
several homes, or a few homes spread out over a large
area—or a whole small town. Or maybe your neighborhood is one floor of the apartment building
you live in. Draw a square for each home
or apartment. In each square, write
the names of the people and
pets who live there. (If you're
an animal lover, you
might know the names
of pets but not their
people!) Are there
any blank squares?
What can you and
your family do to
fill them in?

**Plan to Help a
Neighbor or Two.**
Over dinner, while
you're riding in the car, or whenever your family is
together, share what you've noticed about your neighbors. Who could use some help with yard work? With
grocery shopping? Whose fence needs painting? Who
might like to read the daily newspaper when your

family is through with it? Does anyone need a dog walker? Come up with other ideas and pick one to try.

TiP: A neighborhood event is a perfect time for neighbors to exchange names and phone numbers—great to have in emergencies.

Brainstorm Ways to Bring Your Neighbors Together. What about a block party? A neighborhood clean-up? A potluck picnic? A pet parade? A garden tour? Go with a parent to ask the neighbors next door or across the street if they want to help.

Invite a Neighbor to Dinner. See if your dad or mom is up for having a neighbor eat over. Then, next month, invite a different neighbor. You and your family might enjoy this so much that you make it a tradition. Ask two neighbors who don't know each other and introduce them. Keep the meal simple so you can do some of the cooking.

5 Ways to Be a Good Neighbor

1. Smile and say hi to neighbors you know when you see them on the street, on the sidewalk, in the hall, or at the corner store.

2. When you're watching TV or listening to music, keep the volume down.

3. Never throw litter on the sidewalk or street. Put it in a public trash bin or bring it home.

4. Think about the places at your home that your neighbors can see—a yard if you have one, a porch, a driveway, a deck or balcony, the door to your apartment. Do your part to keep these areas looking neat and clean.

5. If you walk your dog around the neighborhood, remember to clean up the you-know-what. Would YOU want to step in it?

AT SCHOOL

★ If you're asked to do an interview for a school project, interview a neighbor. Choose someone you and your parents already know or want to know better.

★ Invite neighbors you know to plays, concerts, and other special events at your school.

IN YOUR NEIGHBORHOOD

★ Learn the names of younger kids in your neighborhood. Say hi to them when you see them, and greet them by name.

★ If you notice that a neighbor needs help—for example, carrying groceries or getting a stroller through a door— offer to help. You'll make that person's day.

IN YOUR FAITH COMMUNITY

★ Talk with your religion class or youth group about being a good neighbor. Ask your religious leader to give a sermon on this topic. Tips and ideas could be posted on the bulletin board or published in the weekly bulletin.

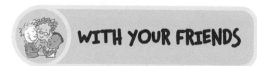

WITH YOUR FRIENDS

★ When you're out together, show respect to all of your neighbors—little kids, teenagers, grown-ups, and seniors.

★ Spend time with younger kids in your neighborhood. They will *love* spending time with you. Play games together, watch videos, or help them with their homework.

★ As a group, offer to help one or more neighbors who could use a hand. You might rake a yard, pull weeds, or carry out trash. Don't take any money for your work.

Start Adding!

Pick at least ONE idea you've read here and give it a try. Then think about or write about what happened. Will you try another idea to help create a more caring neighborhood?

Back to
Lucia's
Story Lucia decides to talk to her parents about how she feels.

"Mom, Dad, I really miss the old neighbors," she says. "I miss Mrs. Alvarez, my old babysitter. I'm scared to start in the after-school program instead of going to her house, like I did before. Plus I don't have any friends here."

Her parents understand completely. "We miss the old neighborhood, too," Lucia's dad admits. "Maybe we can come up with some ideas to help everyone feel a little better."

Lucia's mom goes first. "We could write a 'We're Here!' letter to send to our old friends and neighbors," she says. "We could include a picture of ourselves standing in front of our new house. And we could ask everyone to write back."

"What about a 'We're Here!' party for the people on our new block?" her dad asks. "That's a way to let everyone know we want to make friends."

"We could have a barbecue," Lucia offers.

"Great idea!" her parents say together. "We could invite the families on either side of our new house," her dad suggests. "And a few of them across the street," her mom adds.

Lucia and her parents also agree to go together, knock on every door of each house on the block, and say, "Hi! We're your new neighbors." Lucia figures that meeting and greeting everyone will be a good first step.

"Okay, I'm ready," she says. "Let's go!"

Caring School Climate

What it means: You get along well with teachers and other kids at your school. You feel that school is a caring, encouraging place to be.

Zach's Story

Zach loves his school, and he has a lot of friends there. He knows he's kind of popular, not just with the other kids but with teachers and even the principal. Maybe it's because Zach's dad is the gym teacher, and having his dad at the school helps Zach feel connected. Or maybe it's because Zach tries to be friendly to everyone, even the kids he doesn't know too well.

One day, Zach's teacher comes to him with an idea: "Zach, what would you think about being our Welcome Wagon?"

Zach looks at her and says, "Huh?"

His teacher laughs. "A new girl is joining our class tomorrow. I was hoping you'd be the one to show her around and introduce her to other kids in the school."

Zach immediately agrees.

Zach has the *Caring School Climate* asset.

Facts!

Kids with the *Caring School Climate* asset:

✔ are happier in school

✔ do better in school

✔ score higher on reading and math tests

Think about your own life. Do you feel that your school is a caring, encouraging place to be?

If **YES,** keep reading to learn ways to make this asset even stronger.

If **NO,** keep reading to learn ways to add this asset to your life.

You can also use these ideas to help add this asset for other people—like your friends, family members, neighbors, and kids at school.

Ways to Add This Asset

 **AT HOME**

★ Make a list of adults at school who show they care about kids. How do they show it? Talk with your parents about ways to thank these adults at school. Maybe you or your parents could write each one a thank-you note. Maybe you could write the notes together.

 **AT SCHOOL**

Just Say Yes. If a teacher asks you to try out for the school play, say yes. If a coach invites you to join a team, sign up. If someone suggests that you write for the school paper, give it a try. Make the most of what your school offers. You'll feel more *a part of* school, less *apart from* school. You'll also get to know new people—both kids and grown-ups. *Bonus:* This may help you add the *Other Adult Relationships* asset to your life. See pages 32–42.

Set a Good Example. Don't just wish your school were more caring. Help make it that way. Be someone that other kids look up to and want to be like. How? Try to show a positive attitude about your school and the people in it.

6 Ways to Be More Caring at School

1. Respect school property. Don't be a litterbug.

2. Learn the names of as many other people as you can—kids and adults. Say hi and greet them by name when you see them—in school and out of school.

3. Be friendly to kids who seem lonely or who don't fit in.

4. When you're choosing teams for games, sports, or projects, don't just pick your pals.

5. Be a joiner. Get involved in clubs and groups that work to make your school better.

6. Be a leader. Run for office in a class or school election.

Be a Peer Helper. *Peers* are people from the same age group or place. You and the other kids in your class or grade at school are peers. If your school has a peer-helping program, get involved. (Sometimes these are called peer mediation programs.) Kids in these programs are trained to help other kids by listening to them, offering support and encouragement, and solving problems. Being a peer helper is a great way to be more caring and practice your peacemaking skills. Plus peer helpers get respect.

Show Spirit. Building school spirit isn't just for cheerleaders—anyone can do it. It's great to support your school's teams, but you can also support your school in general. Find new ways to use the school slogan, song, cheer, or symbol. If your school doesn't have any of these, talk with a teacher and the principal about creating them. How about a school-wide contest so students can send in ideas? Winners could get free T-shirts printed with the school slogan and symbol.

IN YOUR NEIGHBORHOOD

★ If you go to school in your neighborhood, let your neighbors know about school events. You might write a School News flyer and hand it out. Even if you don't go to school in your neighborhood, your can still support your neighborhood school. Go to school plays and concerts. (Many are free!) Pick up litter you see on the school grounds.

IN YOUR FAITH COMMUNITY

★ Do the kids in your religion class or youth group go to many different schools? If so, compare experiences. Whose school seems most caring? Why? Are there any ideas you can bring back to your school?

WITH YOUR FRIENDS

★ When you're with your friends, don't trash-talk your school. Try to find something good to say about it. *Examples:* "Lunch wasn't TOO bad today, was it, guys?" "One thing that's fun about school is we all get to see each other, right?" Even if it seems cool to disrespect your school, that doesn't make things better.

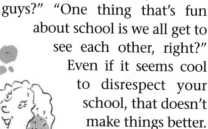

Start Adding!

Pick at least ONE idea you've read here and give it a try. Then think about or write about what happened. Will you try another idea to make your school a more caring place to be?

Back to Zach's Story   Zach comes to school extra early. He wants to be waiting when the new girl, Angie, arrives. He meets her in the principal's office, where her dad brings her on his way to work. She looks kind of shy when she walks in the door. But as soon as Zach goes up to her and says, "Hi! I'm Zach! Are you Angie?" she smiles.

"I'm your Welcome Wagon," Zach explains. "I'll be with you all day. I'll make sure you know where things are and how things work. I'll introduce you to the kids in our class, and other kids, too. And if you need help after today, you can always ask me."

This last part is Zach's idea. Why should a welcome be one day long? It takes more than that to feel comfortable in a new school.

"That would be great," Angie says. Zach can tell she feels better already.

The day goes well. By mid-morning, Angie has three new friends who want to sit with her at lunch. By the end of the day, she's smiling all the time.

"This Welcome Wagon thing really works," Zach thinks. "Maybe we should do it for the whole school, not just our classroom." He decides to ask the principal if the school can start a club that makes new kids feel welcome.

"Sure, why not?" the principal says. "But a club needs a leader. Are you willing to do the job?"

"Yes," Zach answers, "but I'll need help. I think I'll ask Angie. She knows what it's like to be the new kid in school—she *is* the new kid in school!"

The principal nods her head. "Sounds like a plan to me."

The next day, the principal mentions the new club over the loudspeaker during morning announcements. Zach and Angie spend recess time making a sign-up sheet. Zach hangs it on the bulletin board by the office. Five more students sign up right away.

Parent Involvement in Schooling

What it means: Your parents are actively involved in helping you succeed in school.

Aisha & Grace's Story

Aisha invites her new friend Grace to her house for the first time. When they get off the bus, Aisha's mom is waiting for them.

"Oh!" says Grace. "I recognize you from school."

"Yep," says Aisha's mom. "I'm a volunteer. I'm usually there a few times every week."

Inside the house, they all sit at the kitchen table and have a snack.

Aisha's mom asks the same question Grace's dad always asks: "How was school?" To Grace's surprise, Aisha doesn't mumble "Fine" and go back to her snack. Instead, she tells her mom about most of the stuff that happened that day.

Aisha describes the icky burgers they ate at lunch, the bright pink lipstick that Ms. Jenkins (the principal) wore, and which people in their class had a new crush. Aisha's mom laughs, then gets a serious look on her face.

"You haven't said anything about the test you had on state capitals," she asks. "How'd it go?"

"Wow," Grace thinks. "Aisha's mom really knows what's up."

Aisha has the *Parent Involvement in Schooling* asset. Grace wishes she did, too.

Facts!

Kids with the *Parent Involvement in Schooling* asset:

✔ do better on all kinds of tests in school

✔ have fewer learning problems

✔ have better school attendance

Think about your own life. Are your parents (or other family grown-ups) actively involved in helping you succeed in school?

If **YES**, keep reading to learn ways to make this asset even stronger.

If **NO**, keep reading to learn ways to add this asset to your life.

You can also use these ideas to help add this asset for other people—like your friends, family members, neighbors, and kids at school.

ways to Add This Asset

 **AT HOME**

Give Your Parents the 411. When they ask, "How was school?" don't just answer, "Okay, fine, whatever." Really tell them what your day was like, with the nitty-gritty details. Bring home extra copies of your class newsletter or school paper for them to read. Tell them what you heard on the morning announcements.

Encourage Your Parents to Get to Know Your Teacher(s). It's possible you spend more time with your regular classroom teacher than you do with your parents. This is a grown-up who has a big influence on your life. It's someone your parents ought to know! Also, it's good for teachers to know your parents. This helps them understand *you* better.

6 Ways Parents Can Get to Know Teachers

Share this list with your parents.

1. Speak with your child's teacher in person at least once during the school year.

2. Check in with the teacher every other month, either with a phone call or by email.

3. Invite your child's teacher to dinner at your home.

4. Send occasional notes to your child's teacher about things you like—things he or she is doing right.

5. Try never to miss a parent-teacher conference. If you have to miss one, try to reschedule it.

6. Try to attend school events where your child's teacher is sure to be—like the annual open house.

Beg Your Parents to Volunteer at Your School. Or maybe you don't have to beg—your dad or mom might just jump at the chance to get involved. Most schools offer lots of different choices for parents. If your parents can't volunteer during the school day, they can get involved in other ways. *Examples:* They might join the parent-teacher organization. Or serve on a committee or task force that meets in the evenings. Or help out with projects as needed.

Plan Ahead. When you get a school calendar, give it to your parents right away. Offer to write important events on the family calendar. Then you can all plan to attend. Tell your parents that you really want to go to school games, plays, and concerts—and that you need help with rides and tickets. Remind them of special events a few days in advance.

A message for you

If your parents can't come to a school event, see if another grown-up can. What about a grandparent? An aunt or uncle? A cousin? A neighbor? A family friend? An older sister or brother? Don't worry about not showing up with one or both parents. Your friends and teachers will be glad to see you anyway. If an event is especially for parents and kids (like a Mother-Son Breakfast or a Father-Daughter Picnic), ask your teacher if it's okay to bring someone else. This usually isn't a problem.

Deliver the Letter—the Sooner the Better. Don't forget to deliver notes and papers your teacher sends home for your parents to read. Put them in your backpack as soon as you get them (or as soon as you can). Then empty out your backpack when you get home from school.

TiP: Don't wait until the very last minute to ask for help, especially for a big project. This can drive parents crazy.

Ask for Help. Are you stuck on a homework problem? Stumped by a school project? Ask your parents for help. Most moms and dads enjoy giving their kids a hand. They may not know all the answers, but they may have access to the Internet or other ways of getting you what you need.

AT SCHOOL

★ Make your school parent-friendly. Be polite to parents who visit or volunteer at your school. Smile, give a wave, or say hello.

★ Work with teachers and other adults to plan a special event to honor parent volunteers. What about a breakfast, a dinner, or an awards celebration? Or how about something as simple as a thank-you card made and signed by the class?

IN YOUR NEIGHBORHOOD

★ Invite neighbors you know to get involved in your school. Many schools need adult tutors, classroom aids, and other helpers. You don't have to be a parent of a child in that school to lend a hand—and be appreciated.

IN YOUR FAITH COMMUNITY

★ Talk with your youth group or religion class about ways to get parents more involved at your school. What has worked for other kids? Write down ideas to bring home and share.

WITH YOUR FRIENDS

★ Notice and welcome each other's parents when they visit your school. Show them a cool project you're working on. Thank them for coming.

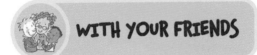

★ Do you and your friends go to different schools? Invite a friend— and his or her parents—to a special event at your school. Then offer to go to an event at your friend's school.

Start Adding!

Pick at least ONE idea you've read here and give it a try. Then think about or write about what happened. Will you try another idea to get your parents more interested and involved in your school life?

Back to
Aisha &
Grace's
Story
Grace reaches for another cookie. She's listening carefully to the conversation between Aisha and her mom.

"I think the test went really well," Aisha says. "I didn't know every answer—I forgot the capital of North Carolina—but I think I got the rest right. Or most of the rest."

"That's terrific," Aisha's mom says. Then she looks at Grace. "Did you take the same test?"

"Yes," Grace mumbles through a mouthful of cookie. She's surprised that Aisha's mom would ask about her day, too.

"Well, how did it go for you?" Aisha's mom wants to know.

Grace swallows her cookie. "Um, not so great, I guess." Because Aisha's mom seems genuinely interested, she decides to open up a bit more. "I'm having trouble reading maps and remembering state and capital names. So I'm not doing so well in geography. . . . But I like spelling a lot. And I'm doing okay in math. I guess my biggest problem at school is staying organized."

"Yeah," Aisha chimes in, "you should see her backpack!"

"Okay, let's see it!" Aisha's mom says.

Soon, all three are looking through Grace's backpack. It's half unzipped, with wrinkled papers poking out. The bottom is a mess of old pencils, gum wrappers, and crumbs.

"Hmmm—this looks serious," Aisha's mom says with a smile. "If you want, I can help you get more organized. I help lots of kids with this at school already. I can even give your dad some tips on helping you keep track of school assignments. Do you think he'd be okay with that?"

"Actually," Grace says, "I think he would. He always asks me about school, but I guess I don't say much. Sometimes I think I'll be bugging him if I ask for help. Or I worry that he'll be disappointed in me."

Aisha's mom reaches over and pats Grace's hand. "It sounds like your dad really cares about you," she says. "I bet he'd be pleased if you'd give him the chance to get more involved."

Grace promises herself that when she gets home, she'll tell her dad all about school—this time in detail.

A NOTE TO GROWN-UPS

Ongoing research by Search Institute, a nonprofit organization based in Minneapolis, Minnesota, shows that young people who succeed have specific assets in their lives—**Developmental Assets** including family support, a caring neighborhood, integrity, resistance skills, self-esteem, and a sense of purpose. This book, along with the other seven books in the **Adding Assets Series for Kids**, empowers young people ages 8–12 to build their own Developmental Assets.

But it's very important to acknowledge that building assets for and with young people is primarily an *adult* responsibility. What kids need most in their lives are grown-ups—parents and other relatives, teachers, school administrators, neighbors, youth leaders, religious leaders, community members, policy makers, advocates, and more—who care about them as individuals. They need adults who care enough to learn their names, to show interest in their lives, to listen when they talk, to provide them with opportunities to realize their potential, to teach them well, to give them sound advice, to serve as good examples, to guide them, to inspire them, to support them when they stumble, and to shield them from harm—as much as is humanly possible these days.

This book focuses on six of the 40 Developmental Assets identified by Search Institute. These are **External Assets**—positive experiences kids receive from the world around them. The six external assets described here are called the **Support Assets.** Support is a fundamental environmental "nutrient." Without it, kids are insecure, isolated, and afraid. With it, they're stronger, more confident and competent, and socially and emotionally healthier.

Young people who have the support assets have positive, fulfilling relationships with many adults—in their families, schools, neighborhoods, and faith communities. These are relationships they can count on, and they know it. How wonderful it is to have people in your life who are there for you, no matter what. How safe and secure you feel. This is what we adults give kids when we build the support assets.

A list of all 40 Developmental Assets for middle childhood, with definitions, follows. If you want to know more about the assets, some of the resources listed on pages 86–87 will help you. Or you can visit the Search Institute Web site at *www.search-institute.org.*

Thank you for caring enough about kids to make this book available to the young person or persons in your life. We'd love to hear your success stories, and we welcome your suggestions for adding assets to kids' lives—or improving future editions of this book.

Pamela Espeland and Elizabeth Verdick
Free Spirit Publishing Inc.
217 Fifth Avenue North, Suite 200
Minneapolis, MN 55401-1299
help4kids@freespirit.com

The 40 Developmental Assets for Middle Childhood

EXTERNAL ASSETS

SUPPORT

1. **Family support**—Family life provides high levels of love and support.
2. **Positive family communication**—Parent(s) and child communicate positively. Child feels comfortable seeking advice and counsel from parent(s).
3. **Other adult relationships**—Child receives support from adults other than her or his parent(s).
4. **Caring neighborhood**—Child experiences caring neighbors.
5. **Caring school climate**—Relationships with teachers and peers provide a caring, encouraging school environment.
6. **Parent involvement in schooling**—Parent(s) are actively involved in helping the child succeed in school.

EMPOWERMENT

7. **Community values children**—Child feels valued and appreciated by adults in the community.
8. **Children as resources**—Child is included in decisions at home and in the community.
9. **Service to others**—Child has opportunities to help others in the community.
10. **Safety**—Child feels safe at home, at school, and in her or his neighborhood.

BOUNDARIES AND EXPECTATIONS

11. **Family boundaries**—Family has clear and consistent rules and consequences and monitors the child's whereabouts.
12. **School boundaries**—School provides clear rules and consequences.
13. **Neighborhood boundaries**—Neighbors take responsibility for monitoring the child's behavior.
14. **Adult role models**—Parents(s) and other adults in the child's family, as well as nonfamily adults, model positive, responsible behavior.
15. **Positive peer influence**—Child's closest friends model positive, responsible behavior.
16. **High expectations**—Parent(s) and teachers expect the child to do her or his best at school and in other activities.

CONSTRUCTIVE USE OF TIME

17. **Creative activities**—Child participates in music, art, drama, or creative writing two or more times per week.
18. **Child programs**—Child participates two or more times per week in cocurricular school activities or structured community programs for children.
19. **Religious community**—Child attends religious programs or services one or more times per week.
20. **Time at home**—Child spends some time most days both in high-quality interaction with parent(s) and doing things at home other than watching TV or playing video games.

COMMITMENT TO LEARNING

21. **Achievement motivation**—Child is motivated and strives to do well in school.
22. **Learning engagement**—Child is responsive, attentive, and actively engaged in learning at school and enjoys participating in learning activities outside of school.
23. **Homework**—Child usually hands in homework on time.
24. **Bonding to adults at school**—Child cares about teachers and other adults at school.
25. **Reading for pleasure**—Child enjoys and engages in reading for fun most days of the week.

POSITIVE VALUES

26. **Caring**—Parent(s) tell the child it is important to help other people.
27. **Equality and social justice**—Parent(s) tell the child it is important to speak up for equal rights for all people.
28. **Integrity**—Parent(s) tell the child it is important to stand up for one's beliefs.
29. **Honesty**—Parent(s) tell the child it is important to tell the truth.
30. **Responsibility**—Parent(s) tell the child it is important to accept personal responsibility for behavior.
31. **Healthy lifestyle**—Parent(s) tell the child it is important to have good health habits and an understanding of healthy sexuality.

SOCIAL COMPETENCIES

32. **Planning and decision making**—Child thinks about decisions and is usually happy with the results of her or his decisions.
33. **Interpersonal competence**—Child cares about and is affected by other people's feelings, enjoys making friends, and, when frustrated or angry, tries to calm herself or himself.
34. **Cultural competence**—Child knows and is comfortable with people of different racial, ethnic, and cultural backgrounds and with her or his own cultural identity.
35. **Resistance skills**—Child can stay away from people who are likely to get her or him in trouble and is able to say no to doing wrong or dangerous things.
36. **Peaceful conflict resolution**—Child attempts to resolve conflict nonviolently.

POSITIVE IDENTITY

37. **Personal power**—Child feels he or she has some influence over things that happen in her or his life.
38. **Self-esteem**—Child likes and is proud to be the person he or she is.
39. **Sense of purpose**—Child sometimes thinks about what life means and whether there is a purpose for her or his life.
40. **Positive view of personal future**—Child is optimistic about her or his personal future.

Helpful Resources

Books

Free to Be You and Me: And Free to Be...a Family (25th Anniversary Edition) by Marlo Thomas (Philadelphia, PA: Running Press, 1998). Stories, songs, poems, and pictures in a fun-filled book for kids and their families.

Reaching Your Goals by Robin Landew Silverman (New York: Franklin Watts, 2004). To turn a wish into a goal takes creative thinking and organized planning skills. This book shows how to make a plan and see it through to the end.

Stick Up for Yourself! Every Kid's Guide to Personal Power and Positive Self-Esteem by Gershen Kaufman, Ph.D., Lev Raphael, Ph.D., and Pamela Espeland (Minneapolis: Free Spirit Publishing, 1999). It's not always easy to say what's on your mind. With a focus on thinking positively and communicating emotions, this book includes tips and exercises to build confidence and make good choices.

Think for Yourself: A Kid's Guide to Solving Life's Dilemmas and Other Sticky Problems by Cynthia MacGregor (Toronto: Lobster Press, 2003). Daily problems are broken down into easy-to-follow categories: friends, family, grown-ups, and everyday situations. Real-life examples and choices for solutions reinforce the importance of thinking things through and doing what's best for you.

Web sites

Family Games
www.familygames.com
A great place to find fun, nonviolent games, quizzes, and software. Downloads are available plus links to more games, riddles, puzzles, and activities the whole family can enjoy.

National Youth Leadership Council (NYLC)
www.nylc.org
The NYLC is working to redefine the role of youth in society by uniting kids, educators, and community leaders to make sure that kids are seen, heard, and actively involved in community organizations and decision making.

Youth as Resources (YAR)
www.yar.org
Kids really can make a difference. YAR supports youth-led service projects, from juvenile justice to public housing and any issue that motivates kids to make our world a better place. Find a YAR program near you, or start your own.

Youth Service America
www.servenet.org
A helpful national resource to connect to organizations and service projects in your area. Type in your ZIP code, skills, and interests to find the best service experience for you.

Books

365 Ways to Raise Great Kids: Activities for Raising Bright, Caring, Honest, Respectful and Creative Children by Sheila Ellison and Barbara Ann Barnett (Naperville, IL: Sourcebooks, Incorporated, 1998). A resource for parents and educators filled with engaging, creative ways to help build self-esteem and strength of character in children.

Building Assets Is Elementary: Group Activities for Helping Kids Ages 8–12 Succeed by Search Institute (Minneapolis: Search Institute, 2004). Promoting creativity, time-management skills, kindness, manners, and more, this flexible activity book includes over 50 easy-to-use group exercises for the classroom or youth group.

Our Family Meeting Book: Fun and Easy Ways to Manage Time, Build Communication, and Share Responsibility Week by Week by Elaine Hightower and Betsy Riley (Minneapolis: Free Spirit Publishing, 2002). Time management, long-range planning, and prioritizing skills are important assets for busy families. This book keeps many schedules organized and promotes open, effective communication within families.

Parents Do Make a Difference: How to Raise Kids with Solid Character, Strong Minds, and Caring Hearts by Michele Borba (New York: Jossey-Bass, 1999). Based on nationwide research and pilot programs in elementary schools, this book combines simple steps to reinforce positive self-esteem in kids.

What Kids Need to Succeed: Proven, Practical Ways to Raise Good Kids by Peter L. Benson, Ph.D., Judy Galbraith, M.A., and Pamela Espeland (Minneapolis: Free Spirit Publishing, 1994). More than 900 specific, concrete suggestions help adults help children build Developmental Assets at home, at school, and in the community.

What Young Children Need to Succeed: Working Together to Build Assets from Birth to Age 11 by Jolene L. Roehlkepartain and Nancy Leffert, Ph.D. (Minneapolis: Free Spirit Publishing, 2000). Communicating, mentoring and instilling confidence in adolescents is no small task. Based on significant research and analysis, this guide includes creative, constructive ways to build a firm foundation for children from day one.

Web sites

Alliance for Youth
www.americaspromise.org
Founded after the Presidents' Summit for America's Future in 1997, this organization is committed to fulfilling five promises to American youth: Every child needs *caring adults, safe places,* a *healthy start, marketable skills,* and *opportunities to serve.* This collaborative network includes resources, information, and opportunities for involvement.

Connect for Kids
www.connectforkids.org
This site provides tips, articles, resources, volunteer opportunities, and more for adults who want to improve the lives of children in their community and beyond. Includes Richard Louv's *101 Things You Can Do for Our Children's Future.*

National Mentoring Partnership
www.mentoring.org
A wealth of information about becoming and finding a mentor, this organization provides connections, training, resources, and advice to introduce and support mentoring partnerships.

Search Institute
www.search-institute.org
Through dynamic research and analysis, this independent nonprofit organization works to promote healthy, active, and content youth and communities.

Index

About the Authors

Both Pamela Espeland and Elizabeth Verdick have written many books for children and teens.

Pamela is the coauthor (with Peter L. Benson and Judy Galbraith) of *What Kids Need to Succeed* and *What Teens Need to Succeed* and the author of *Succeed Every Day*, all based on Search Institute's concept of the 40 Developmental Assets. She is the author of *Life Lists for Teens* and the coauthor (with Gershen Kaufman and Lev Raphael) of *Stick Up for Yourself!*

Elizabeth is a children's book writer and editor. She is the author of *Teeth Are Not for Biting, Words Are Not for Hurting,* and *Feet Are Not for Kicking* and coauthor (with Marjorie Lisovskis) of *How to Take the GRRRR Out of Anger* and (with Trevor Romain) of *Stress Can Really Get on Your Nerves* and *True or False? Tests Stink!*

Pamela and Elizabeth first worked together on *Making Every Day Count.* They live in Minnesota with their families and pets.

Books from Free Spirit

Helping Out and Staying Safe
The Empowerment Assets
by Pamela Espeland and Elizabeth Verdick
The second book in the "Adding Assets" Series
for Kids introduces and describes the four
empowerment assets: Community Values
Children, Children as Resources, Service to
Others, and Safety. Kids learn simple, everyday
ways to play useful roles at home and in the
community, help others, and feel safer at home,
at school, and in the neighborhood. For ages
8–12. *$9.95; 96 pp.; softcover; two-color illus.; 5⅛" x 7"*

*To place an order or to request a free catalog of SELF-HELP FOR KIDS®
and SELF-HELP FOR TEENS® materials, please write, call, email,
or visit our Web site:*

Free Spirit Publishing Inc.
217 Fifth Avenue North • Suite 200 • Minneapolis, MN 55401-1299
toll-free 800.735.7323 • local 612.338.2068 • fax 612.337.5050
help4kids@freespirit.com • www.freespirit.com

What's faster, friendlier, and easier to use?
www.freespirit.com

New
look

New
features

New
sections

More
ways to
search

Quicker
check-
out

Stop in
and see!

Our fresh new Web site makes it easier than ever to find the positive, reliable
resources you need to empower teens and kids of all ages.

For a fast and easy way to receive our practical tips, helpful information,
and special offers, send your email address to e-news@freespirit.com.

1.800.735.7323 • fax 612.337.5050 • help4kids@freespirit.com